Review of Tom Bower book
Revenge: Meghan, Harry and the war
between the Windsors

Ethon Noah

D1526916

Table of contents

Chapter 1

As I report this adventure, many individuals have needed reality when they realized they were being misled. However many falsehoods have been taken care of to general society and concealed, and the issue with lies is that it leaves a path that doesn't make any sense. This book has professed to have addressed the individuals who have stayed quiet, may be out of dread, since they were paid off, or hushed through an NDA. It is not yet clear who has stood up, and what they have said. A key individual would be Ninaki Priddy, who was hushed right off the bat, and who was unloaded by her previous dearest companion when she called TW out on a few awkward unpleasant realities.

The title of the book (REVENGE) represents itself with no issue in that it creates the impression that Harry and TW (that spouse) have been looking for 'vengeance' against the British Royal Family since they didn't get what they requested. This proceeds right up to the present day, and one of the issues is the hesitance to eliminate or do whatever it takes to eliminate the ducal title, hence, each time the pair play up and mishandle the title for financial addition, the RF can fault themselves for the hopelessness and shame they cause to themselves and the world. By neglecting to eliminate the titles, the RF embarrass themselves each time they permit the couple to utilize the title, either to elevate themselves or to bring in cash.

The new declaration that Harry (with TW close by obviously) will give some sort of discourse on Nelson Mandela day on 18 July 2022 at the UN has been portrayed as more than it is. Could he have been approached to talk (or maybe he has paid to talk with an enormous gift?) assuming the title had been stripped because that could have sent an unmistakable message that the RF had banished him and decreased his status? Who believes that a shamed imperial should talk at their occasion?

The court issues proceeds (prevarication has no time limits), TW is being sued by her sister, Harry is seeking a lawful test against the Government (guaranteeing his 'quick line of progression' status qualifies him for police security and if the state won't pay, he cases ought to be permitted to pay for the assistance, realizing without a doubt that can never occur), and Harry is guaranteeing that the Mail on Sunday slandered him for deluding explanations (that seem to have been given by his PR group).

In some way or another, he appears to have failed to remember that he harmed his standing with deluding and wrong articulations and claims made during the Oprah Winfrey interview in 2021. General society didn't have to peruse the Mail on Sunday to conclude their thought process of Harry, as they saw and heard Harry shame himself with his own words during that meeting. Attempting to fault a paper when you harmed your standing (yet don't wish to recognize it) is unimportant and presumptuous, and to fault it because of the remarks segment is ridiculous. Peruse the remarks on any article on the team (whether positive, nonpartisan, or pessimistic) on any news site and there will be a large number of pessimistic remarks from genuine individuals (not bots).

It is to be sure difficult to monitor every one of the tricks that the couple pulls, and keeping in mind that BP and KP might have disguised a few awkward mysteries when these mysteries have hurt others, (for example, the claims of harass which seem to have validity), then, at that point, there is an ethical obligation to confess all. That is, assuming the government wishes to hold the trust and steadfastness of the People it claims it serves.

One forsaken excuse of a man and his ongoing spouse does not merit tossing hundreds of years of unwaveringly and regard away, yet that is where we are present. The Platinum Jubilee that the pair guaranteed they were eager to go to bring about booing and sneers, yet they just went on two occasions and one was away from plain view. They decided not to go to public family occasions, and nobody missed them or minded.

I expect an outburst of deflective Sussex PR turned articles throughout the following week and on the delivery date of the book of 21 July 2022, where a couple of faithful allies of the pair will give interviews on any individual who will tune in. Individuals/noble causes will post spouting remarks on their virtual entertainment records to redirect from the book, however, let us see who has stood up and whether it will prompt a #MeToo development, where individuals will at long last stand up after being harassed into quiet. Will it will enable other 'casualties' to talk about their reality with the goal that they can mend and continue?

A touchy new book asserts that the Queen let her staff know that she was appreciative Meghan Markle didn't go to Prince Philip's burial service. Notable biographer Tom Bower has written the book, which is called Revenge Meghan, Harry and the conflict between the Windsors.

The creator claims that she told her helpers upon the arrival of the memorial service: "Thank heavens". Sovereign Philip's memorial service, on April 17, 2021, denoted a month since Prince Harry and Meghan's great meeting with Oprah Winfrey and a year since the Sussexes had ventured down from their imperial obligations.

Nook composes that the state of mind was "grave" as the media lauded Philip's life in front of his burial service at St George's Chapel, Windsor. The Sun reports that he stated: "The practices showed perfect military drill. Few wouldn't be moved by the flawlessness of British stylized custom. The weather conditions were conjectured to be extraordinary.

Meghan Markle and Prince Harry's crack with the Royal Family is such a ton more profound than anybody envisioned - - basically as indicated by another detailed storybook, which has the supposed tea.

Celebrated creator Tom Bower - - known for his memoirs about the Royals, the majority of which are not endorsed by the subjects - - has an impending venture hitting racks called "Retribution: Meghan, Harry and the conflict between the Windsors" ... also, kid, does he get into it.

Per Bower ... There were unobtrusive shots taken between the two players in secret and a few fights these previous small bunch of years ... which appears to have originated from Meghan's Vanity Fair cover in 2017, whenever she first openly recognized the relationship.

It was a generally little piece of the article, with Meghan saying ... "We're a couple, we're enamored," and proceeding to say they'd ultimately approached and recounted their story in full. Yet, VF's title was about their relationship - - "She's Just Wild About Harry!"

Obviously, as per Bower, the Royals were pissed - - because they'd explicitly trained Meghan NOT to discuss Harry. At that point, they'd been seen together freely, however, neither had addressed the press. Meghan, thus, allegedly got quite agitated with her PR office ... advising them to request VF pull the statement and change their point. Vanity declined.

Chapter 2

That doesn't appear to have had an incredible effect with Buckingham Palace - - as we probably are aware, strains just developed as time continued ... arriving at an edge of boiling over with the Oprah interview.

The result of that plunk down ended up being wrecking, so says Bower - - proved in Queen Elizabeth II supposedly expressing something with the impact of ... "Thank heavens Meghan isn't coming," when Prince Philip kicked the bucket a month after the meeting circulated. MM was pregnant again at that point ... also, just Harry went to the memorial service, yet even he was said to have been restless while there.

When Lilibet was conceived ... there were reports that Meghan and Harry sprung the name (Liz's genuine moniker) on the Queen - - which Bower likewise clearly affirms in his book.

At long last, there's the show that was very clear at the Queen's Platinum Jubilee recently - - when Harry and Meghan were more than a safe distance from the remainder of the family all through their whole time there ..., particularly for the sought after gallery seating.

It just so happens, as per Bower, MM and PH were hell-bent on getting a spot close to the Queen - - this, Bower claims, as a trade-off for what they assumed they were owed for acquiring the children out there the primary spot - - however Prince Charles shut it down ... what's more, the Queen unobtrusively cosigned by not allowing their desires. As you most likely are aware, Harry and Meghan left a short time later.

There's additionally the issue of Prince Harry's meeting with Hoda Kotb, where he somewhat dissed his sibling and father - - while causing it to seem like he and nana were maybe considerably nearer than she was with any of her different youngsters/grandchildren. The Royals detested this as well, Bower claims.

There's significantly more that is to come in the genuine book. 'Vengeance' drops Thursday.

As summer arrives at its level in the UK and Europe, a large number of individuals are taking off holiday or removing a period from work to find companions and family members.

Also, that incorporates the royals. July and August are normally calm for a very long time in the imperial schedule, as individuals from the family enjoy some time off from their weighty timetable of public obligations.

Unexpectedly, the traveling and chaotic schedule of public appearances, addresses, and illustrious visits stops — and individuals go off-lattice.

Be that as it may, how simple is it for the regal family to genuinely move away from everything - and what occurs on an imperial occasion?

The most popular holiday spot for the royals is Balmoral Castle in Scotland, where the Queen spends her summers and where various family social gatherings have occurred.

Diana and Prince Charles partake in a mid-year occasion in Majorca on board King Juan Carlos of Spain's yacht in 1990. Credit: Getty

While at Balmoral, the ruler has envisioned getting a charge out of nation strolls, riding ponies, and facilitating picnics with her loved ones. "It's the most gorgeous put on the planet ... and I think Granny is generally cheerful there," Princess Eugenie said in a 2016 ITV narrative.

In any case, royals likewise hope to go further away from home. The Queen's late sister, Princess Margaret, spent extended vacations on Mustique, an island in Saint Vincent, and the Grenadines in the Caribbean.

Her association with the island started in 1960 when she saw it while cruising the Caribbean on the imperial yacht, Britannia. Its proprietor, Colin Tennant, gave her a 10-section of a land plot as a wedding present, and she later involved her island estate as a retreat from the glare of the media and to have gatherings in the organization of famous people.

Numerous royals have likewise been inclined toward a chilly climate retreat. Sovereign Philip took his kids Princess Anne and Prince Charles on a skiing excursion to

Liechtenstein in 1965, and Diana, Princess of Wales consistently treated her young men William and Harry to certain experiences on the slants.

What's more, at times, sentiment prospers during imperial escapes. At the point when Prince Harry presented Meghan Markle as his life partner in 2017, he educated journalists regarding their heartfelt excursion to Botswana, where they set up camp under the stars, away from meddlesome eyes.

That visit was a significant one for the couple. Their time in the nation was even addressed on Meghan's wedding band, which highlighted a jewel from the southern African country.

Harry's heartfelt story isn't unlike that of his sibling, William, who proposed to Kate

Middleton during an escape at a log lodge in the shadow of Mount Kenya. The couple got drawn in while remaining at a natural hideout close to a rambling creature save where rhinos and giraffes meander openly.

With such countless recollections made while secretly visiting the world, it's little marvel the royals value their days off as much as most of us.

Last December, William, and Kate set a photograph free from their vacation to Jordan. We don't yet have the foggiest idea where the royals are setting out toward their excursions this year, yet after a bustling period over the Queen's Jubilee weekend last month, there's presumably they'll appreciate setting up their out-of-office messages.

It's not been a decent couple of days for the Royal Family. In seven days the government machine would be overwhelmed by festivities for the Duchess of Cornwall's 75th birthday celebration and all-around profound respect for her acts of kindness.

He added: "It has gone out to be... an extremely hard trudge since individuals were hesitant to talk and she and her attorneys had done very well to keep individuals quiet, yet I got past [to] enough.

"Furthermore, it's an extraordinary story. A shocking story of a lady who came from nothing and is presently a world figure and has stomped all over every one of those others on the way which is exemplary for the kind of individuals I generally pick, whether it's a legislator or a big shot. The casualties are quick to talk and they have spoken. Furthermore, it's a true story."

Arbor gave no sign whether the "people in question" he discussed were the castle staff who Meghan was blamed for harassing or individuals from additional back in her biography.

The Duchess of Sussex was blamed for driving two PAs out of the imperial family in a 2018 email from her correspondence secretary Jason Knauf to an unrivaled in Kensington Palace. Meghan denies the charges.

The first, epic and genuine story of the Duke and Duchess of Sussex's coexistence, at long last uncovering why they decided to seek a more free way and the explanations for their uncommon choice to move back from their illustrious lives, from two top regal correspondents who have been in the background since the couple initially met. Finding Freedom is finished with the full variety of photos from Harry and Meghan's romance, wedding, Archie's achievements, and a lot more extraordinary minutes.

Interestingly, Finding Freedom goes past the titles to uncover obscure subtleties of Harry and Meghan's coexistence, dissipating the many tales and misguided judgments that plague the couple on the two sides of the lake. As individuals from the select gathering of columnists that cover the British Royal Family and their commitment, Omid Scobie and Carolyn Durand have seen the two or three lives a couple of pariahs can.

"Retribution: Meghan, Harry and the War between the Windsors," will be one that Meghan Markle is fearing, basically as per a source who talked with the distribution. "Tom doesn't go easy and is frighteningly exhaustive in his exploration. No stone will be left unturned," the source added.

"Tom Bower, Britain's driving insightful biographer, unpicks the tangled web encompassing the Suffixes and their relationship with the regal family. From court dramatizations to subject governmental issues, utilizing broad exploration, master obtaining, and meets from insiders who have never spoken, this book reveals a surprising story of affection, disloyalty, mysteries, and retribution"

Made in the USA
Monee, IL
18 July 2022

99962671R00015